The SIMPLY wonderful

cook book

recipes by
Heather Robinson

A LION BOOK
Oxford · Batavia · Sydney

LION

Published by
Lion Publishing plc
Sandy Lane West, Oxford, England
ISBN 0 7459 2204 X
Albatross Books Pty Ltd
PO Box 320, Sutherland, NSW 2232, Australia
ISBN 0 7324 0565 3

First edition 1992

Acknowledgments
Studio photography by John Williams Studios, Thame.
Illustrations by Helen Herbert
Additional photographs:
Robert Harding Picture Library 3; Nick Rous 4, 5 (top);
ZEFA (Jörg Trobitzsch 5 (bottom); Harry Smith Horticul-
tural Photographic Collection 7, 11.
A catalogue record for this book is available
from the British Library

Library of Congress CIP Data applied for

Printed and bound in Singapore

**Many thanks to all the cooks who peeled,
chopped, grated, mixed, stirred and tasted
to make sure that these recipes were simply
wonderful.**

*Theo Addae, Rosalind Cuthbert,
Sharon V. Cuthbert, Carley Dolton,
James Fletcher, Kerry Gardner,
Steven Philip James, Alexander J. Leggate,
Edmund Robinson, Jonathan Robinson,
Daniel Rock, Davina Rock, Sebastian Rock,
Tony Wake, Annaly Faith Watkins,
Heidi Watkins, Annalee Webb.*

**Younger children may need
grown-up supervision when
cooking.**

CARE FOR THE WORLD...
and enjoy great food

This is a book to enjoy. It's simply packed with recipes that you can use to make good food for yourself, your friends and your family. All the recipes have been tested by young people, and we included only the ones where the majority vote was that the result tasted great!

However, there's more to good food than just yumminess. Good food is food that makes your body grow strong, and that means getting a balance of different types of foodstuffs: protein for growth, fat and carbohydrate for energy, fibre to help your bowels work, plus essential vitamins and minerals for radiant health. If you choose a balance of foods from the four main food groups, you are almost certain to be getting all these nutrients. Look for these symbols next to the recipes to help you choose:

 Fruits and vegetables

 Breads and cereals

 Dairy produce

 Protein foods

The recipes chosen are also kind to the world. All the food that we have depends on the miracle of the natural world. Sunlight makes green plants grow, providing leaves, stems, roots, seeds and fruit for us and other animals. We  need to be kind to the atmosphere, the soil, the plants and the animals if we want to have a continuing supply of food. This book suggests several ways in which you can help.

The recipes use lots of fresh, natural ingredients. This in itself makes the most of what the world has to offer. It also cuts down on the amount of expensive food processing that is needed, on the amount of transport that is needed to race food to your local shops, and on the amount of packaging required to keep foods in good condition.

The recipes provide foods that make you feel warm and comfortable inside, but they are not about being greedy. If you are able to use the recipes in this book, that also means you are able to get your hands on to—and your teeth into—quite a lot of food. Many people in this world do not have enough to eat. Those of us who have enough need to find ways to eat more simply, as a first step to sharing the world's resources more fairly.

This book is also about celebrating! Sharing food with people can be a very practical way of showing that you love them. It might be a simple family meal or a splendid party: it's the good time you can have together that matters.

In many ways all this is just good sense. Many people in the world today care deeply about the Earth and the people on it. However, the people who wrote this book did so for a special reason: we all believe that the world was made by God, and that people were put in charge of the creation, to use it wisely, carefully, and for the good of all. We want you to care for the world and enjoy good food because we think that's getting back to God's plan! And as you know if you've tried to use any delicate piece of machinery, it's a good idea to follow the maker's instructions: they are there to help and protect us.

CONTENTS

A Great Start! 1

Shake Up, Shape Up 2

Spice of Life 3

The Lunch Factory 4

Dairy Delight 5

Nutty Ideas 6

Pick Your Own Meal 7

Midsummer Madness 8

Autumn Abundance 9

The Complete Homeburger 10

In the Soup 11

Winter Warmers 12

The Hungry Gap 13

Parties! 14

Totally Cool 15

Ice-cream Parlour 16

Disposable Dishes 17

Christmas Celebrations 18

Easter Treats 19

Gift of Food 20

A Great Start!

Get your day off to a great start with a healthy breakfast. It looks good, it tastes good, and it's easy to make enough for everyone in your household!

FRUIT GONDOLAS

One melon will make four or six gondolas. If you don't want so many, you can keep the remaining melon, lightly wrapped in plastic, in the fridge for a day.

chopping board
sharp knife
teaspoon
colander

1 melon (honeydew or cantaloupe)
100 g strawberries

1 On the chopping board cut the melon in half lengthways and scoop the seeds out with the teaspoon. Then cut each half into two or three wedges.

2 Wash the strawberries in the colander and shake them dry. Hull the strawberries by cutting out the green bit and the hard 'core' underneath. Cut each in half.

3 Arrange the strawberries to look like passengers in a gondola-style boat.

Choose summer fruits when they are in season in your part of the world. Think of different combinations of fruits to put in your gondolas that taste good and that make the most of what grows locally.

GOLDEN MUFFINS

This amount makes 12 medium-sized muffins. They are good to eat plain, and are great spread with butter or margarine!

small bowl
large mixing bowl
whisk
mixing spoon
muffin tin
paper cases
tablespoon

100 ml orange juice
50 g sultanas
50 ml sunflower oil
150 ml clear honey
1 egg
150 g self-raising flour
100 g wholemeal self-raising flour

Pre-heat the oven to 180°C.

Arrange the paper cases in the muffin tin.

1 Put the orange juice and sultanas in the small bowl and leave to soak for about 15 minutes.

2 Put the oil, honey and egg into the large bowl. Whisk together to make a smooth, thick mixture. Stir in the orange juice and sultanas.

3 Add the two sorts of flour and stir into the mixture very lightly. It is better to leave the mixture a little bit lumpy than to stir it too hard.

4 Put a spoonful of the mixture into each paper case and bake for 12–15 minutes.

Add some protein to your breakfast with a glass of milk. Skimmed milk contains all the goodness of whole milk, but less fat—and who wants more of that?

Shake Up, Shape Up

Whizz together a healthy breakfast with these two recipes.

BANANA FOAM

The quantities here are enough for one drink, but no doubt other people in your family will want some.

blender
sharp knife
large tumbler

1 banana
300 ml milk, chilled
5 ml honey
1–2 ml lemon juice, to taste

Check that you are allowed to use the blender, and follow the instructions for its use exactly.

1 Peel the banana and slice the fruit carefully into the blender.

2 Add the milk, honey and lemon juice. Blend for one minute until smooth and frothy.

3 Serve immediately in a large tumbler.

OATIES

mixing bowl
mixing spoon
5 ml sunflower oil
2–3 baking trays
wire rack

100 g margarine
125 g brown sugar
1 egg
5 ml hot water
1 ml vanilla essence
75 g self-raising flour
75 g wholemeal self-raising flour
50 g chopped almonds or hazelnuts
75 g rolled oats

Lightly grease the baking trays with the sunflower oil.

Pre-heat the oven to 170°C.

1 Put the margarine and sugar in a bowl and beat together until smooth and creamy.

2 Add the egg, hot water and vanilla essence and mix again.

3 Stir in the two types of flour until well mixed, then stir in the chopped nuts and rolled oats.

4 Take spoonfuls of the mixture about the size of a walnut. Place them on the baking trays, at least 5 cm apart, and then flatten them slightly with your hand.

5 Bake for 10 minutes. Leave to cool on the tray for about 2 minutes, then lift the cookies off to finish cooling on a wire rack.

There are all kinds of crunchy bars and biscuits you can buy... but do you really need the pretty packaging? You throw it away so soon and it uses up valuable resources. Make your own unwrapped version with these Oaties. The recipe makes about 24. They keep well in an airtight tin, or you can freeze them in a reusable plastic box. Just take out what you need.

Spice of Life

Here's a wonderfully warming winter breakfast. You can make your own breakfast bread using the recipe on page 4.

Dried fruit is a traditional winter standby. The fresh fruit is dried on racks, perhaps in the harvest sun. As the water evaporates and the fruit shrivels, the sugars left behind become more concentrated. This concentration of sugar stops bacteria growing, and the dried fruit lasts a long time. It's better value than fresh fruit out of season, which either has to be grown in artificial heat or transported quickly from a long way away. Both methods can use up the world's fossil fuels.

FRUIT SOUP

You need to start this recipe a night and a full day before you want to eat it. These quantities are enough for 4–6 people.

kitchen scissors
measuring jug
mixing bowl
large saucepan with lid
fine grater
small chopping board
sharp knife
lemon squeezer
mixing spoon
serving bowl and plate to cover

100 g dried figs
100 g dried apricots

100 g large raisins
100 g prunes
750 ml cold water
1 orange
425 g yoghurt
50 g toasted almonds or hazelnuts, chopped

1 Snip the figs in half. Then place the apricots, raisins, prunes and figs in a large bowl and cover with about 750 ml water. Adjust the amount as necessary to make sure that all the fruit is covered. Leave to soak overnight.

2 Pour away 75 ml of the water. Place the fruit and remaining water in the saucepan. Heat on the top of the stove till the water is just boiling.

3 Put the lid on, turn the heat down and leave to simmer for about 10 minutes, or until the fruit is soft.

4 Meanwhile, grate the orange rind on the chopping board. Cut the orange in half and squeeze out the juice.

5 Lift the saucepan carefully on to a heatproof work surface. Add the rind and juice and stir well with the mixing spoon.

6 Pour the fruit soup into a serving bowl. Cover with the plate, allow to cool and then chill in the refrigerator.

7 Serve with yoghurt and chopped toasted nuts.

★ The yoghurt topping adds protein to this breakfast.

Dried fruit doesn't contain all the vitamins in fresh fruit. The luxury addition of orange juice adds a dash of vitamin C, as well as extra delicious flavour.

CINNAMON BUNS

bread knife
cutting board
baking tray
fine grater
small saucepan
mixing spoon

6 bread rolls
1 lemon
60 g butter
60 g soft brown sugar
10 ml cinnamon
2 ml nutmeg

Pre-heat the oven to 180°C.

1 Lay each roll on its side and use the bread knife to make 2 cuts in each. Cut only 3/4 of the way down so that the bread still holds together. Put the bread on the baking tray.

2 Grate a little lemon rind into the pan. Add the butter, sugar, cinnamon and nutmeg.

3 Heat gently on the top of the stove. When the butter has melted, carefully lift the pan on to a heatproof work surface. Stir gently with the mixing spoon.

4 Spoon a little of the mixture between each of the slices. Then bake the cinnamon bread in the oven for 8 minutes. Serve immediately.

The Lunch Factory

It's fun to pack a portable meal, for lunch or for a picnic. Of course, you can buy all kinds of tempting goodies ready to go... but think again. So many of them are wrapped in plastic and foil packaging that you only use once. Often the food has to contain preservatives to stop it going off. Why not make your own lunch foods, using the recipes from the next three pages?

BASIC BREAD

Bread is basic to many portable meals. You can make loaves and slice the bread to make sandwiches, or make rolls that you stuff with your favourite fillings... or just plain good bread that you tear off in chunks and eat!

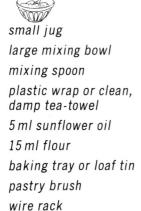

small jug

large mixing bowl

mixing spoon

plastic wrap or clean, damp tea-towel

5 ml sunflower oil

15 ml flour

baking tray or loaf tin

pastry brush

wire rack

450 ml warm water

10 g dried yeast

15 ml soft brown sugar

350 g wholemeal flour

350 g strong white flour

10 ml salt

25 g margarine or butter

a little extra flour

5 ml oil

Pre-heat the oven to 200°C for rolls, or 220°C for a loaf, when you reach the second stage of kneading.

Rub oil over the inside of your baking tray or loaf tin and dust lightly with a little flour.

1 Put a little of the water into the small jug and gently stir in the sugar and yeast. Leave for 5 minutes or until frothy.

2 Put the two types of flour into a bowl and stir in the salt.

3 Rub the margarine or butter into the flour, using your fingertips to break it into tiny pieces.

4 Stir the yeast liquid into the dry ingredients and add enough of the remaining water to make a firm dough that leaves the bowl cleanly.

5 Sprinkle a little extra flour on a clean work surface and tip the dough on to it. Knead firmly, pushing down with the heel of your hand and folding the dough over, until it is no longer sticky.

6 Wash out the mixing bowl and dry thoroughly. Oil the inside lightly, then add the kneaded dough. Cover the bowl with plastic wrap or a clean, damp tea-towel and leave to rise in a warm place (such as an airing cupboard) until the dough has doubled in size. This can take up to 2 hours.

7 Sprinkle extra flour on the work surface, tip out the risen dough and knead again.

8 Shape into 12 rolls or 1 large loaf.

SUPER SOFTIES

If you like soft rolls, this is the recipe for you. Super Softies make great hamburger buns, too. You follow the same instructions as for basic bread rolls, but use a milk-and-water mixture instead of plain water, and slightly different proportions.

150 ml milk
150 ml hot water
5 ml dried yeast
15 ml soft brown sugar
150 g wholemeal flour
300 g strong white flour
5 ml salt
50 g margarine or butter
a little extra flour

1 After the second kneading stage, divide the dough into 8–10 pieces. Shape each into a ball and flatten slightly before leaving them to prove.

2 When you take the baps out of the oven, wrap them in a clean, dry tea-towel and leave to cool. The moisture trapped inside the tea-towel keeps the crust soft.

Keep bread fresh by freezing it in a re-usable plastic box. Take out only what you need.

After the loaf has risen again, brush with beaten egg and sprinkle with poppy seeds or rolled oats.

Brush this knot with salt water made from 10 ml salt in 30 ml water.

Snip the dough to make prickles on a hedgehog roll. Brush the prickles with beaten egg after it has risen.

9 Place dough in the baking tray or loaf tin, cover with plastic wrap or the damp tea-towel and leave to rise for about 30 minutes or until doubled in size. (The loaf will need about 1 hour to rise.)

10 Remove the covering and bake the rolls for 15–20 minutes, the loaf for 30–40 minutes.

11 Carefully remove from the oven and leave to cool. After 2 minutes, turn the bread on to a wire rack to cool.

★ Try the double-decker from the front cover, with crisp, fresh lettuce, sliced tomatoes and red pepper, and your choice of cold meat and sliced cheese.

Rippling golden waves of ripening wheat are a beautiful sight and a promise of food in abundance. Wholemeal flour uses all the goodness of the grain, providing fibre that helps your body process its food and also giving you some extra nutrients. White flour makes softer, lighter breads and cakes. Try using different proportions of wholemeal and white flour when you bake, to find what suits you best.

Dairy Delight

Set up your own dairy to make yoghurt and soft cheese. The milk used to make both of these is full of protein.

Several animals produce enough milk for humans to be able to milk them successfully... not just cows and goats, but also sheep and reindeer!

YOGHURT PLANT

Friendly bacteria are what turns milk into smooth, creamy yoghurt. These bacteria need to be kept nice and cosy, so make sure you get the temperature right.

large saucepan
thick casserole with lid
spoon
towel or blanket

15 ml plain yoghurt
450 ml milk

Check with a grown-up that it is all right to use a towel or blanket, and agree with them on the best place in which to leave your yoghurt to grow.

1 Pour the milk into a large saucepan. Bring to the boil on the top of the stove. Just as the milk begins to bubble, turn the heat down and let the milk simmer gently for 2 minutes.

2 Allow the milk to cool for about 30 minutes. Wash your hands before testing the temperature: put your finger in the milk and begin counting. Take your finger out as soon as the milk feels too hot. When you can keep your finger in comfortably for a count of 10 the milk is at the right temperature (about 45°C).

3 Use the spoon to lift any skin off the milk.

4 Put the plain yoghurt into a thick casserole and stir till smooth. Then add the milk, a little at a time, and stir till thoroughly mixed.

5 Put the lid on the casserole, wrap in the towel or blanket and put in a warm place such as an airing cupboard.

6 Leave for 8 hours or overnight. Carefully unwrap and lift the lid, but try not to shake the liquid or it won't set. If it is not set, rewrap and leave for a couple of hours longer.

7 When the yoghurt is set, store it in the refrigerator.

★ You can keep a couple of tablespoons of your home-made yoghurt to start your next batch.

★ For a portable meal, pack a small amount of yoghurt in a reusable plastic pot with a lid that stays on firmly. If you like fruity yoghurt, add a spoonful of jam—perhaps the raspberry jam described on page 6. Be sure to wash out the yoghurt container at the end of the day.

CHEESE MACHINE

sieve

*cotton muslin, about
30 cm x 60 cm*

large bowl

homemade yoghurt

1 Fold the cotton muslin in half and use it to line the sieve.

2 Place the sieve so that it rests firmly on the sides of the bowl. Pour in the yoghurt.

3 Put in the refrigerator and leave to drain for up to 24 hours. A thin liquid, the whey, will drain away, leaving a thick, soft cheese in the sieve. The cheese can be kept in a plastic box in the fridge for up to 5 days.

4 You can mix it with all kinds of ingredients to make a scrumptious filling for your homemade rolls or bread.

★ finely chopped pineapple

★ grated orange rind, chopped walnuts and raisins

★ flaked tuna fish and chopped cucumber

★ chopped red or green pepper, with finely chopped spring onions

The process for making hard cheeses begins in much the same way as your cheese machine. More moisture is squeezed out of the cheese, and the solid mass that is left behind is specially treated so that the cheese keeps well. Cheese-making is a technique used all over the world to make the most of milk that can't be used right away.

Nutty Ideas

You'd be nutty not to try these recipes for nutritious nibbles. Nuts contain body-building protein, which is why this book uses them for the protein symbol.

TRADITIONAL ROAST NUTS

Some nuts taste better raw, some taste better roasted, some are simply wonderful however you eat them. Here are three suggestions for nuts that are good roasted.

Dry roasted peanuts are better for you than ones that are roasted in oil.

baking tray

shelled peanuts

Pre-heat the oven to 180°C.

1 Sprinkle the shelled peanuts over the tray. Shake gently until you have a single layer with enough spare room for you to turn the nuts easily without spilling them.

2 Put the tray of nuts in the oven for 20 minutes. Every 5 minutes, lift the tray out and shake it a little so the peanuts roll over.

3 After 20 minutes the peanuts should be brown but not burnt.

★ Try the same recipe with sunflower seeds. Shake them every 3 minutes. They will take about 9 minutes to roast.

★ Almonds are expensive but delicious. Roast them the same way as sunflower seeds.

PEANUT BUTTER

Make your own special brand from peanuts you roast yourself.

blender
2 clean jars with lids
spoon

450 g roasted peanuts
15–30 ml sunflower oil
salt, to taste

Ask a grown-up to help you get the jars really clean.

Check that you are allowed to use the blender, and follow the instructions for its use exactly.

1 Put the nuts in the blender with 15 ml of the oil. Put the lid on carefully, switch on the blender and liquidize until smooth.

2 Switch the blender off, remove the lid and check the peanut butter. If it seems too stiff, add the remaining oil before covering and blending for a couple of seconds more. If it seems too plain, add a little salt.

3 Spoon the peanut butter into the jars and put the lids on. You can store the peanut butter in the refrigerator for up to 2 months.

★ Use roasted sunflower seeds in the same way to make sunflower seed butter.

★ Cashew nut butter is wonderful. Make it with unroasted cashew nuts.

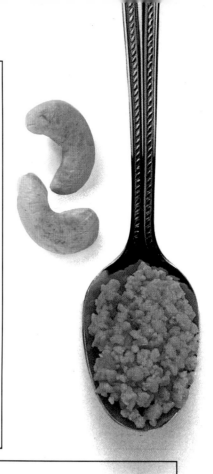

RASPBERRY JAM

Hands up if you think peanut butter tastes better with jam. If that includes you, you'll need this recipe to make your very own PBJ.

You can also enjoy your jam on bread or in yoghurt.

colander
very large saucepan
wooden stirring spoon
small plate
2 or 3 glass jars
wooden board
small jug
wax discs
jam pot covers

450 g raspberries
450 g preserving or granulated sugar

Ask a grown-up to help you get the jars really clean. Then put them in a cold oven and set the heat at 100°C to warm the jars gently.

The jam froths up in the pan when it cooks. Ask a grown-up to help you select a saucepan big enough so that the fruit and sugar will only half fill it.

1 Wash the fruit in a colander and drain.

2 Put the fruit in the large saucepan and heat gently until the juices flow.

3 Let the fruit boil for about 5 minutes until soft. Carefully pour the sugar into the saucepan. Stir with the wooden spoon until the sugar is thoroughly dissolved.

4 Bring the mixture to the boil and boil for 5 minutes without the lid on.

5 Carefully lift the pan off the heat. Spoon a small amount of the jam mixture on to the plate and allow to cool for a minute. Then push the surface gently with your finger. If it crinkles, it means the jam is beginning to set. If it doesn't, put the pan back on the heat and boil for 2 more minutes, then test again.

6 Wear oven mitts to lift the jars out of the oven onto a wooden board. Dip the jug into the jam and pour it, a little at a time, into the jars, filling them up to the neck.

7 Seal each jar with a wax disc. Leave to cool, and then cover.

Jam making is a traditional way to preserve the summer harvest of fruits. The sugar is needed to stop the fruit going bad – but go easy on how much you eat, or you'll get fat!

Pick Your Own Meal

What do you fancy eating for your main meal today? Sometimes there's so much to choose from, you find it hard to decide.

Usually the cheapest food—and the best—will be what's being harvested in your area. There's lots of it, and it can be brought to you quite fresh.

If you have a garden you may even be able to grow your own.

Here's a meal that makes the most of some of the early crops of summer.

You can also grow crops in pots on a sunny window-sill. Tiny tomatoes and peppers do well. Low-growing herbs such as parsley and basil are also happy on a window-sill, and you can snip off a few leaves as you need them.

RATATAT STEW

In the south of France they call it ratatouille—a lovely stew of summer vegetables. Make some for your family.

chopping board
sharp knife
colander
plate
weights, or tin of food
kitchen towel or tea-towel
wooden stirring spoon
large saucepan

2 aubergines
3 courgettes
15 ml salt
2 medium onions
2 cloves garlic
2 red or green peppers
60 ml vegetable oil
450 g tomatoes
15 ml fresh basil
salt and pepper, to taste

1 On the chopping board cut the aubergines and courgettes into 1.5 cm slices. Cut each aubergine slice in half across.

2 Place the slices into a colander and sprinkle with salt. Cover with a plate and place some weights on top. Leave for an hour. This will draw out the juices, which can be rather bitter. Then tip the slices on to kitchen towel or a tea-towel to soak off the moisture that will have formed on each slice.

3 On the chopping board peel and slice the onions, then peel and finely chop the garlic. Cut open the peppers and remove the seeds. Slice the skins.

4 Heat the oil in the saucepan and add the chopped onion. Cook in the oil, stirring lightly with the wooden spoon, for about 8 minutes. Then add the garlic and cook for 2 more minutes.

5 Add the aubergines, courgettes and peppers. Cook gently for 5 minutes, stirring occasionally.

6 Meanwhile chop the tomatoes into quarters on the cutting board and stir in. Chop the basil leaves and add those too. Stir well, sprinkle in some salt and pepper, then cover the pan and leave to simmer for 30 minutes.

Enjoy your stew with homemade bread and your favourite cheese. Alternatively, you can serve it on a bed of pasta sprinkled with grated cheese.

FLOWER POWER SALAD

Here is some of the most colourful food in the world. Eating flowers is an old idea that's coming back into fashion.

Do make quite sure, however, that the flowers you choose are edible ones, and that they have not been sprayed with any garden chemicals.

colander
salad bowl
large bowl
15 ml salt
glass jar with lid
spoon

1 large lettuce

3–4 marigold flowers
(You will need to use the daisy-like pot marigold, not the ruffly sort.)

a few nasturtium leaves and flowers

25 ml olive oil

15 ml lemon juice

10 ml clear honey

salt and pepper, to taste

1 Wash the lettuce and drain thoroughly in a colander.

2 Tear into shreds and put in the salad bowl.

3 Dip the flower leaves and petals in a bowl of cold salted water. Gently shake dry.

4 Tear up the nasturtium leaves and a few of the flower heads and add them to the salad.

5 Decorate the salad with marigold petals and nasturtium flowers.

6 Put the oil, lemon juice, honey, salt and pepper into the jar and shake hard for a minute. Just before you serve the salad, pour some of this dressing over it and toss lightly with a spoon.

★ In spring you can make a flower salad with garden primroses and violets.

Uncooked food contains lots of vitamins and minerals. Try to have some raw vegetables every day.

Midsummer Madness

High summer has to be the best time for fruity desserts. Fresh fruit is naturally sweet, and you can just pick it, wash it and eat it. Or you can slice fresh summer fruits into a bowl to make a marvellous fruit salad.

For a special occasion, you can make something a bit more complicated.

APRICOT TOAST

Day-old bread makes good toast, and is used in this recipe, which makes four servings.

butter knife
baking sheet
sharp knife
teaspoon

4 slices day-old bread
butter
8 apricots
50 g caster sugar

Pre-heat the oven to 140°C

1 Spread each slice of bread with butter, and place butter-side down on the baking sheet. Then butter the top side.

2 Carefully cut each apricot in half and remove the stone. Fill each cavity with a spoonful of sugar, and arrange 4 halves, sugar-side up, on each piece of bread.

3 Place the baking tray in the oven and bake for about 40 minutes. Serve immediately.

★ Make this dessert extra special by using vanilla sugar. You make this by leaving a vanilla pod in a jar of sugar for a few days. You can re-use the pod to flavour many batches of sugar!

RED²

These quantities make about 4 servings. Make it only when summer fruits are in season. You may be in an area where you can pick your own.

colander
sharp knife
chopping board
bowl
large enamel saucepan
sieve
spoon

1 kg strawberries
350 g raspberries
30 ml lemon juice
250 g caster sugar

1 Put the strawberries in the colander and wash under cold running water. Shake dry.

2 Slice each strawberry in half and cut out the hard core. Place the strawberry halves in the bowl.

3 Place the raspberries in the colander and wash under cold running water. Then tip them into the saucepan and add the lemon juice and sugar.

4 Over a low heat, bring the contents of the saucepan to the boil. Stir from time to time. Simmer for 2 minutes.

5 Lift the pan on to a heatproof surface and leave to cool.

6 Place the sieve over the bowl and tip in the raspberry mixture.

Stir with a spoon so that the fruit purée goes through and the pips are left behind.

7 Stir the strawberries and the raspberry mixture together. Chill before serving.

Autumn Abundance

After the spring rain and the summer sunshine the autumn harvest can be enormous—more than anyone could ever eat all at once. But the lean days of winter lie ahead, so it is important to find ways to store the extra food to last through the time when there is very little growing.

Some of the old-fashioned ways of preserving extra vegetables in sugar and vinegar are not really the most nutritious method of keeping them, but the results do taste good.

You can easily buy these two preserves ready-made, but these home-made versions taste even better—and at last you'll really know what goes into them!

For both of these recipes you will need clean, warm glass jars and vinegar proof lids. Ask a grown-up to help you clean the jars properly shortly before you need them. Then put them in a cold oven and warm them through by turning the heat to 100°C. Take them out of the oven and put them on a wooden board only when you are ready to use them.

BETTER-THAN-KETCHUP

sharp knife
chopping board
large saucepan, with lid
spoon
blender
2–3 glass jars and covers

1 medium onion
water
450 g tomatoes
75 g raisins
75 g sultanas
150 g brown sugar
250 ml malt vinegar
2 ml cinnamon
2 ml ginger
5 ml salt
15 ml mustard seeds
1 bay leaf

Be sure to get the jars ready in time.

Check that you are allowed to use the blender, and follow the instructions for its use exactly.

1 Peel and chop the onion. Put it in the saucepan and add just enough water to cover it. Put the lid on the pan, and slowly heat until the water boils. Turn the heat down and leave to simmer for 15 minutes.

2 Meanwhile chop the tomatoes into quarters and cut out the hard part of the core. Add to the pan with all the remaining ingredients. Stir gently as you bring the mixture to the boil.

3 Put the lid on and leave to simmer over a gentle heat for 30 minutes. Then remove the lid and leave to simmer even more gently for about an hour. Stir occasionally, taking great care not to spill any of the hot mixture.

4 Remove from the heat and leave to cool for 15 minutes. Stir until you find the bay leaf, and remove it. Then tip the mixture into the blender and whizz until smooth.

5 Carefully spoon the mixture into warmed jars and cover with vinegar-proof wraps and lids.

SUPER SWEET PICKLE

sharp knife
chopping board
bowl, and plate to cover
colander
large saucepan
spoon
2–3 glass jars and covers

1 large cucumber (about 450 g)
1 medium onion (about 150 g)
15 ml salt
100 g brown sugar
15 ml mustard seeds
2 ml turmeric
1 ml mace
250 ml white wine vinegar

Be sure to get the jars ready in time.

1 Cut the cucumber in half lengthways. Lay one half cut-side downwards on the chopping board and make another lengthways cut. Then chop in 5 mm slices. Repeat with the other half.

2 Peel the onion, cut each in four lengthways, then slice thinly.

3 Put the vegetables into a bowl, and sprinkle with salt. Cover with a plate and leave for 3 hours.

4 Tip the vegetables into a colander to drain, then run cold water all over the vegetables in the colander and drain again.

5 Mix together in the saucepan the brown sugar, mustard seeds, turmeric, mace and vinegar. Bring to the boil, and boil for 2 minutes.

6 Add the drained vegetables and bring to the boil again. Simmer for 5 minutes. Then lift the pan on to a heatproof surface and spoon the mixture into warmed jars. Seal carefully with the vinegar-proof wraps and lids.

The Complete Homeburger

Goodbye mass-produced hamburgers, all guaranteed to taste just as average as the last one. Hello homeburger, designed to suit your tastes.

The traditional Meatburger is very good, and provides a lot of protein. However, producing meat demands a lot of the world's resources. Forests that teem with wildlife may be destroyed to create farmland for raising beef cattle. Many ordinary people who live in those areas may not be left with enough land to grow food for themselves.

Meat is good sometimes. For a change, try a Veggyburger, which helps you to share the world's food resources more fairly.

MEATBURGER

sharp knife
chopping board
bowl
mixing spoon
oil brush
grill pan

450 g ground beef
1 small onion
salt and pepper
30 ml vegetable oil

1 Peel the onion and chop finely.

2 Mix the chopped onion with the beef in a bowl, and add a sprinkling of salt and pepper.

3 To the mixture add some extra flavouring. Here are some to try:

★ 50–100 g grated cheese

★ 15 ml sweet pickle

★ 5–10 ml prepared mustard

4 Mix well together and then with very clean hands shape the mix into 4 flat burgers.

5 Place on a grill rack and brush with oil. Grill for about 5 minutes at medium–high heat, then turn, brush the other side with oil and grill for another 5 minutes.

BURGER ASSEMBLY

How do you like your burger? And how do your mother/father/brother/sister/granny like theirs? Let them build their own with

top slice of bun (Super Softies, of course)

Super Sweet Pickle

sliced cheese

sliced tomato

burger

Better-than-Ketchup

bottom slice of bun

VEGGYBURGERS

The mixture for these is really sticky until it has chilled. Allow yourself plenty of time!

baking tray
knife
chopping board
grater
frying pan
mixing spoon
plate
oil brush
grill pan without rack

20 g sunflower seeds
1 large onion
1 small clove garlic
2 small carrots
1 medium courgette
50 g Cheddar cheese
10 ml sunflower oil
150 g rolled oats
1 small egg
5 ml chopped sage
30 g plain flour
salt and pepper to taste
45 ml extra sunflower oil

Rub a little of the oil over the base of the grill pan.

1 Sprinkle the sunflower seeds on a baking tray and toast under a medium-hot grill for 2 minutes. Shake them, and toast for 2 more minutes.

2 Peel the onion and grate it. Then peel the garlic and grate that separately on the fine part of the grater.

3 Grate the carrots and courgette together.

4 Grate the cheese separately.

5 Heat 10 ml oil in the frying pan. Add the onion and stir gently over a low heat for 5 minutes. Add the garlic and stir for 1 minute more.

6 Add the carrots and courgette and cook for 2 minutes more.

7 Lift the pan on to a heatproof surface and add the toasted seeds, grated cheese and oats. Stir in the egg and sage, add a sprinkling of salt and pepper, and mix well.

8 Chill the mixture in the fridge. It is best if you can leave it for at least an hour.

9 When the mixture is cool, sprinkle some flour on to a plate and season it with salt and pepper. Take a quarter of the mix and roll it in the flour, then flatten it into a burger shape. Make three more burgers in the same way and put them on the oiled grill pan.

10 Brush the burgers with more oil and grill on medium heat for 5 minutes. Then turn them over carefully with a slice, brush with more oil, and grill for 5 minutes longer.

In the Soup

Nothing could be simpler than a bowl of warming vegetable soup, served with lots of freshly-baked home-made bread and some cheese.

You can afford to invite lots of people to enjoy such a good, inexpensive meal, and be generous spending time with them.

These recipes make about 4 servings, but you can easily make more.

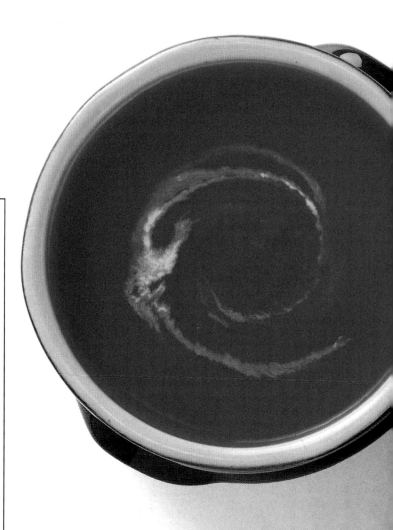

CARROT SOUP

vegetable peeler
sharp knife
chopping board
large saucepan
mixing spoon
large jug
blender

7 medium carrots
1 small onion
25 g margarine or butter
500 ml water
100 ml milk
50 ml single cream
salt and pepper to taste

Check that you are allowed to use the blender, and follow the instructions for its use exactly.

1 Peel the carrots and cut them into 5 mm slices.

2 Peel and chop the onion.

3 Melt the margarine or butter in the saucepan over a low heat. Add the onion and cook, stirring gently, for about 5 minutes.

4 Add the carrots and continue cooking for 2 minutes.

5 Pour in the water. Bring to the boil, then turn down the heat and let the soup simmer gently for about 45 minutes.

6 Lift the pan off the heat. Use the jug to put half the soup into the blender. Liquidize till smooth. Pour the remaining soup into the jug and tip the liquidized soup into the pan. Then liquidize the second batch of soup, and stir that into the pan.

7 Add the milk and cream, and heat through for just a minute. Season with salt and pepper.

Some vegetables last well into cold winters. Root vegetables can be lifted from the soil in which they grew, and stored, either in layers of straw and earth out of doors, or inside in a cool, dark room or a cellar. In both cases they are kept cold but free from frost.

POTATO AND LEEK SOUP

Leeks actually grow through the winter in areas where there isn't too much snow. Use them with stored root vegetables in this soup.

vegetable peeler
sharp knife
chopping board
large saucepan, with lid
stirring spoon
large jug
blender

3 medium potatoes
3 medium leeks
25 g margarine or butter
500 ml water
salt and pepper, to taste
100 ml milk
50 ml single cream

Check that you are allowed to use the blender, and follow the instructions for its use exactly.

1 Peel the potatoes and chop them into cubes.

2 Cut off the green part and the root of the leeks. Slice each piece in half lengthways and wash carefully to get any soil out. Cut into 1 cm slices.

3 Melt the margarine or butter in the saucepan over a medium heat. Add the potatoes and leeks and stir well. Put the lid on the pan, turn the heat down and leave to cook very gently for 10 minutes.

4 Lift off the lid, add the water and some salt and pepper. Turn up the heat and bring to the boil. Then turn the heat down, put the lid back on, and leave the soup to simmer for about 20 minutes, or until the vegetables are tender.

5 Carefully lift the soup off the heat. Use the jug to put half the soup into the blender. Liquidize till smooth. Pour the remaining soup into the jug and tip the liquidized soup into the pan. Then liquidize the second batch of soup, and stir that into the pan.

6 Stir in the milk and cream and put the pan back on the heat for just one minute.

★ Both of these soups look pretty with an extra spoonful of cream swirled into each bowlful, and some chopped parsley sprinkled on top.

Winter Warmers

A simple meal of rice and beans is standard fare in many parts of the world.

Share an everyday feast with millions of ordinary people, as a first step to sharing all the world's resources with them as fairly as possible.

BEANFEAST

This chilli-style meal uses far fewer of the world's resources to produce than a meat dish does, but provides you with a lot of body-building protein.

It's easiest to get the beans cooked the day before you want to make the meal. You can even cook up large quantities of beans and freeze the extra in batches the right size for the next time you want to make the meal.

large saucepans
sharp knife
chopping board
grater
stirring spoon

75 g dried red kidney beans
75 g dried chick peas
75 g dried black-eyed beans
1 large onion
4 cloves garlic
2 carrots

15 ml sunflower oil
20 ml ground coriander
20 ml ground cumin
300 ml yoghurt cheese or soured cream
150 ml water
30 ml chopped parsley

1 Prepare the beans. Wash each sort in a colander, then leave to soak in a pan of cold water. Rinse in the colander again.

2 Put in a large pan, bring to the boil and boil rapidly for 10 minutes. **THIS IS VERY IMPORTANT**.

3 Turn the heat down and leave to simmer until they are soft. Drain in a colander and rinse under cold running water.

4 Peel and chop the onion and garlic.

5 Peel and grate the carrots.

6 Heat the oil in a large saucepan. Add the onion and stir gently over a low heat for about 5 minutes. Add the garlic, carrots, coriander and cumin and cook for 2 minutes, stirring all the time.

7 Add the cooked beans, the yoghurt cheese and the water. Cook gently for 1–2 minutes.

8 Stir in the parsley just before serving.

	Soak	Boil	Simmer
red beans	8 hours	10 minutes	30-40 minutes
black-eyed beans	1 hour	10 minutes	25-30 minutes
chick peas	8 hours	10 minutes	2 hours

NICE RICE

Serve this with the Beanfeast for a complete meal. This is enough for four people.

large saucepan, with lid
spoon
colander

150 g brown rice
1 litre water
15 ml salt

1 Put the water and salt in the saucepan and bring to the boil.

2 Turn down the heat, add the rice and stir round. Put the lid on the pan and simmer for 40 minutes.

3 Put the colander in a clean, empty sink and tip the rice into it. If you wish to get rid of the sticky starch, you can rinse the rice in very hot water, boiled in the kettle.

VITAMIN BOTTLE

The fresh vegetables that provide lots of healthy vitamins can be scarce in winter. Grow some vitamins in a jar by sprouting seeds.

jam jar
sieve
piece of cotton muslin, or any open weave cotton
rubber band

15 ml seeds for sprouting

1 Put the seeds in the sieve and wash them under cold running water.

2 Put them in the jar and just cover with water. Leave to soak.

3 When they have soaked for the time shown in the chart, tip them back into the sieve and rinse under cold running water again.

4 Put them back in the jar, cover the top with muslin and fix this on with the rubber band. Put the jar on its side.

5 Every morning and evening, fill the jar with water through the muslin, then tip upside and allow to drain thoroughly.

★ Add a few sprouted seeds to your beanfeast, a few minutes before the end of the cooking time.

★ Mix beansprouts with grated raw carrot and a few raisins for a side salad to your winter meal.

	Hours soaking	Days growing
chick peas	12	3
alfalfa seeds	7	5
sunflower seeds	12	2

The Hungry Gap

Everyone welcomes the arrival of spring, with buds breaking into leaf and shoots emerging from the soil. However, it is the time when there is very little to eat: most of the winter foods have been used up, and the new harvest is still a long way off. In this hungry time you can treat yourself and your family to some warming desserts made with basic foods that store well: flour, sugar, and stored or dried fruit.

SPICY FRUIT CRUMBLE

sharp knife
chopping board
1 litre oven-proof dish with a lid
2 mixing bowls

675 g cooking apples
75 g soft brown sugar
2 ml ground cloves
30 ml raisins
75 g margarine or butter
175 g wholemeal flour
2 ml ground cloves
50 g soft brown sugar

Pre-heat the oven to 180°C.

1 Carefully peel the apples. Cut each into quarters and remove the cores. Cut each quarter into thin slices and put them in the dish.

2 Mix 75 g brown sugar with 2 ml ground cloves and the raisins. Add to the apples.

3 Put the lid on the dish and place in the oven. Cook for 25 minutes.

4 Meanwhile mix together in a bowl the flour, 2 ml ground cloves and 50 g brown sugar.

5 With your fingertips rub the margarine into the flour until it is in pieces so small that the mixture looks a bit like breadcrumbs.

6 Lift the dish out of the oven and place it on a heatproof work surface. Lift off the lid and sprinkle the topping over the apples.

7 Bake the crumble uncovered for 25 minutes more, then carefully lift it out of the oven.

★ Serve with home-made yoghurt lightly sweetened with sugar or honey, or home-made vanilla ice-cream. See the recipes on pages 5 and 16.

LEMON MYSTERY

Baffle your friends with this intriguing dessert. You mix a smooth, creamy batter and put it in the oven to cook. Out comes a spongy topping with a luxurious lemon sauce underneath.

glass
2 small bowls
grater
2 plates
sharp knife
lemon squeezer
mixing bowl
mixing spoon
whisk
1.5 litre oven-proof dish
5 ml oil
roasting tin
hot water

2 eggs
1 large lemon

50 g margarine or butter
100 g caster sugar
250 ml milk
50 g self-raising flour

Ask a grown-up to help you half fill a roasting tin with hot water, and put it in the oven. Check that you can put the oven-proof dish in it easily when it is in the oven.

Pre-heat the oven to 190°C.

Grease the oven-proof dish with the oil.

1 Break the eggs one at a time onto a plate. Trap the yolk with the glass and tip the white into one bowl. Then tip the yolk into the other.

2 Grate the lemon rind on to a clean plate. Cut the lemon in half and squeeze out the juice into the cup.

3 Put the margarine or butter into the mixing bowl with the sugar and lemon rind. Beat with the mixing spoon until light and fluffy.

4 Add the egg yolks a little at a time, beating well in between.

5 Stir in the milk and lemon juice.

6 Add the flour and mix thoroughly.

7 Whisk the egg whites until they form soft white peaks.

8 Add the egg whites to the lemon mixture and mix them in, lifting and stirring gently.

9 Pour the mixture into the dish. Then place in the roasting tin in the oven and bake for 45 minutes.

10 Lift carefully out of the oven and serve immediately. Turn off the oven, and leave the pan of water inside until it is quite cool.

Parties!

Parties are fun! You can have a good time laughing and letting off some steam with people you really like. At a good party, everyone feels they have friends.

Take care when you organize a party. You know how awful it can be to feel left out. Is there anyone you should invite who doesn't have lots of friends—perhaps someone new to the area, someone who always seems to be on the sidelines? Your party could be the start of lots of new friendships for them.

NIBBLES

Get everyone nibbling while they find things to talk about. Roast nuts and seeds make good nibbles, and roasted without fat are nutritious too. See the recipes on page 6.

CHEESY CRACKERS

bowl
grater
baking tray
greaseproof paper

50 g plain white flour
75 g margarine
75 g cheese
25 g rolled oats or oatmeal

Pre-heat the oven to 200°C.

Line the baking tray with greaseproof paper

1 Put the flour in a bowl and rub in the margarine.

2 Grate the cheese into the bowl, and add the oats.

3 Now mix well with your hands until the mixture forms a single lump of dough.

4 Pull off pieces the size of a walnut and roll them into a ball. Then flatten them on the baking sheet.

5 Bake for 12–15 minutes, until golden brown. Carefully remove from the oven on to a heatproof surface and leave in the tin to cool.

POPCORN

large saucepan, with lid

15 ml sunflower oil
50 g popping corn
salt

1 Heat the oil in the saucepan until it begins to sizzle.

2 Drop one bit of corn into the pan. When it pops, the temperature is right.

3 Add the rest of the corn and put the lid on quickly.

4 Turn the temperature down to low and shake the pan every few seconds as the corn pops. Keep doing this till the corn stops popping.

5 Sprinkle with a little salt to serve as a party snack.

FOSSIL FLOATIES

Trap the natural wonders of your century in ice... and then float them on your lemonade, or any other cool drink that you serve.

ice cube tray

jug

water

glacé cherries

tiny curls of orange or lemon rind

sprigs of mint

edible flower heads or petals (borage, violets)

1 Make your choice of ingredients to freeze, then arrange them as you want in each ice cube compartment.

2 Gently pour water from your jug into each compartment and freeze.

LEMONADE

Talking is thirsty work. Make sure there is lots of lemonade to drink.

vegetable peeler

large bowl

plate to cover bowl

spoon for stirring

sharp knife

chopping board

lemon squeezer

sieve

large jug

3 lemons

175 g granulated sugar

50 g pearl barley (optional)

900 ml boiling water

1 Use the vegetable peeler to pare off a thin layer of the yellow peel from each lemon (avoid the white part underneath). Place in the large bowl.

2 Add the sugar, and pearl barley if you are using it.

3 Pour on the boiling water, stir with the spoon, then cover and leave for a few hours. Stir the mixture occasionally.

4 Cut each lemon in half and squeeze out the juice. Add the juice to the bowl.

5 Strain the lemonade through a sieve into a large jug and serve.

SPICY SAUCE

This sauce goes with everything savoury at your party. Making the mayonnaise bit is particularly impressive!

sharp knife
chopping board
lemon squeezer
frying pan
spoon for stirring
sieve
medium bowl
small bowl
small jug
small mixing spoon

1/2 small onion
1 clove of garlic
1 lemon
30 ml sunflower oil
15 ml curry powder
150 ml tomato juice
1 egg yolk
150 ml extra sunflower oil
50 ml natural yoghurt
150 ml double cream
salt and pepper, to taste

1 Chop the onion and the clove of garlic very finely. Cut the lemon in half. Squeeze one half, and cut a slice from the other.

2 Put 30 ml oil in a frying pan and stir the onion over a low heat until soft but not coloured. This will take about 5 minutes. Add the garlic and stir for 1 minute.

3 Add the curry powder and cook for 1 minute more.

4 Add the tomato juice and lemon slice, and a sprinkling of salt and pepper.

5 Cook over a low heat for 8 minutes. Leave the pan without a lid on so that some of the liquid will evaporate.

6 Carefully lift the pan off the heat. Place the sieve over the bowl, and strain the pan liquid

through. Throw away the bits that won't go through, and leave the rest to cool.

7 Meanwhile make some mayonnaise. Put the egg yolk in a small bowl and the 150 ml oil in a small jug. Mix the egg yolk very well then slowly add the oil, a drop at a time, stirring hard between each drop.

8 Once you have put in half the oil, add the lemon juice and stir again. Then add the remaining oil, about a teaspoon at a time, until it is all used up. The result should be very thick and creamy.

9 Stir the mayonnaise, yoghurt and cream into the cool curry mixture and check the taste. Add a little more salt and pepper if you wish.

PARTY PLUSSES

Make a rice salad for your guests. Cook some brown rice, as described on page 12, and rinse it in cold water. Let it drain and add chopped red pepper, a few cooked peas, chopped spring onions and some salt and pepper. A sprinkling of chopped parsley looks nice.

Raw vegetables look bright and colourful, and they're good to eat. Chop cucumber, pepper and carrots into thin sticks, and break broccoli into small florets. Arrange them on a plate.

SURPRISE EGGS

saucepan
serving bowl

8 eggs
1/2 quantity spicy sauce

1 Put your eggs in the saucepan, and add enough cold water to cover them.

2 Bring the water to the boil over a high heat, then turn the heat down and let the water simmer for about 8 minutes.

3 Carefully lift the pan off the heat and tip the water away. Take care not to tip the eggs out! Then fill the pan with cold water to cool the eggs.

4 After a minute or so the eggs will be cold enough to handle easily. Crack the shells and peel them away.

5 Slice the eggs and put them in a serving bowl. Pour over the spicy sauce.

SAUCY CHICKEN

baking tray
skewer
plate
sharp knife
bowl

50 g butter
4 large chicken joints
salt and pepper, to taste
1/2 quantity spicy sauce

Pre-heat the oven to 180°C

1 Rub a little of the butter over the bottom of the baking tray.

2 Wash each joint under cold running water, then shake dry and lay on the tray, skin side up.

3 Sprinkle each joint with a little salt and pepper and dot small blobs of butter on each.

4 Bake for about 25 minutes, then lift on to a heatproof work surface. Poke the thickest part of the meat with a skewer. If clear juices run out, the chicken is done. If not, spoon a little melted butter over the pieces and put the whole tray back in the oven for about 10 minutes, then test again, and cook just a little longer if necessary.

5 When the chicken is done, leave to cool. Then cut the meat off the joints and put in a serving bowl. Pour the spicy sauce over.

Ice-cream Parlour

Is it true that everyone likes ice-cream? It must be one of the most popular desserts there are. Set up a little ice-cream parlour at your party, and let your guests help themselves to a scoop of ice-cream all full of the goodness of milk and guaranteed free from unwanted additives.

Well, ice-cream actually contains a lot of fat and sugar too, which is not strictly good for you if you eat too much of it, but for a party...

VERY VANILLA

whisk
large bowl
2 litre freezer container
strong spoon and fork for stirring

300 ml double cream
225–350 g sugar (more or less according to taste)
600 ml whole milk or semi-skimmed milk
2 ml natural vanilla essence

1 Whip the cream until it forms soft peaks.

2 Stir in the sugar and the vanilla essence.

3 Slowly stir in the milk until evenly blended.

4 Pour the mixture into the freezer container and place in the freezer. Check after 2 hours, by which time the mixture should have begun to freeze round the edges.

5 Remove from the freezer and stir the frozen parts into the unfrozen part till it is smooth and slushy throughout. Put back in the freezer.

6 After 2 more hours, stir in the same way again, until it is slushy. Then put back in the freezer and freeze until firm.

7 Remove from the freezer and keep in the fridge for about half an hour before serving.

★ Find out how to make vanilla sugar on page 8. If you use vanilla sugar, you can skip the vanilla essence!

CHOCOLATE LEAVES

This is a really glamorous decoration for your ice-cream.

small bowl

large bowl

rose leaves or fresh bay leaves

baking tray

greaseproof paper

75 g chocolate

The leaves need to be washed well in advance, so they have time to dry completely.

1 Break the chocolate into the small bowl.

2 Put a little hot water in the large bowl and stand the small bowl in it. The water needs to come above the level of the chocolate in the small bowl. Add more water if you need to, but be very careful not to splash any water into the chocolate as even a drop will spoil it.

3 Line the baking tray with greaseproof

paper. Gently dip the backs of the leaves in the chocolate and place carefully, chocolate-side up, on the baking tray.

4 Place the tray of leaves in the refrigerator for at least 30 minutes, until the chocolate is quite hard again.

5 Carefully peel off the leaves.

STRAWBERRY ICE

sharp knife

blender

bowl

whisk

1 litre freezer container

spoon and fork for stirring

450 g strawberries

1 ml lemon juice

125 g caster sugar

300 ml double cream

Check that you are allowed to use the

blender, and follow the instructions for its use exactly.

1 Carefully cut the hard core out of each strawberry.

2 Put the strawberries in the blender and liquidize.

3 Add the lemon juice and sugar to the strawberries.

4 Put the cream in the bowl and whisk until it forms soft peaks.

5 Gently stir in the fruit until the

mixture is evenly pink.

6 Pour into the freezer container and freeze for 2 hours. Remove from the freezer and stir until slushy throughout.

7 Put back in the freezer and freeze until firm.

Serve your ice-cream with fresh fruit, such as blueberries, orange segments, sliced peaches and some chopped nuts, so your guests can construct their own glorious dessert. The raspberry sauce used with strawberries (page 8) is also very good with ice-cream.

Disposable Dishes

Look at any fast-food restaurant and see the amount of WASTE they create: all those handy throw-away packs use up natural resources at a horrific rate.

But washing up can be dull, so it's tempting to use throw-aways when you have a party.

Solve the problem with a party that uses naturally disposable dishes!

You'll need a wipe-clean table to put the food on, and spoons to eat the mousse with.

These quantities are enough for eight people.

SUNSHINE PIZZAS

Begin by making one batch of bread, using the basic bread recipe on page 4. Oil and flour 3 large baking trays. Divide the dough into eight pieces and shape each into a pizza about 20 cm in diameter. Now make the topping.

oil brush

knife, for spreading

grater

sharp knife

chopping board

baking trays

15 ml sunflower oil

120 ml tomato puree

2 large red peppers

8 green olives

150 g cheese

100 g extra cheese

Pre-heat the oven to 210°C.

1 Brush the top of each pizza with a little oil.

2 Spread a little tomato paste over the top of each.

3 Grate 150 g cheese and sprinkle over each pizza. Press down gently.

4 Cut the red peppers open and remove the seeds. Cut the red skin into small triangles. Arrange them round the edge of each pizza.

5 Add olive slices for the eyes, and add a piece of red pepper at the centre of each.

6 Use small pieces of red pepper to make a smiley mouth.

7 Arrange the pizzas on baking trays. Cook for about 15 minutes.

8 Meanwhile, cut the remaining cheese into slices, and cut the slices into triangles.

9 Wear oven mitts to lift the baking trays on to a heatproof surface. Quickly arrange cheese triangles around the edge to look like the sun's rays. Return to the oven for 2–3 minutes, until the cheese just bubbles.

VEGETABLE DIP

bowl
fork
sharp knife
chopping board

250 g yoghurt cheese or cottage cheese
60 ml mayonnaise
salt and pepper, to taste
8 small red or orange peppers
2–3 carrots
1 cucumber

1 Put the yoghurt cheese in a bowl and mix in the mayonnaise and a little salt and pepper.

2 Neatly cut each pepper in half as shown to give you two cup-shaped pieces. Carefully cut the seeds and white parts out of each.

3 Peel old carrots, or simply wash new ones, and carefully cut into sticks. Peel or wash the cucumber. Cut into sticks.

4 Put a few of each kind of vegetable into the stem half of each pepper. Put a little of the cheese mixture in the bottom half of the pepper.

5 Your guests begin by dipping their carrot and cucumber sticks in the dip to eat, then they can dip the empty half, and finally eat the rest of the pepper.

★ Make a flavoured dip, using one of the sandwich spread ideas on page 5.

CHOCOLATE ORANGES

grater
2 plates
glass
1 small bowl
1 medium bowl
2 large bowls
orange squeezer
whisk
teaspoon

4 large oranges
175 g plain chocolate
3 eggs
15 ml single cream

1 Make sure the oranges have been washed and dried, then grate a little rind from the stem end and the opposite end of each on to the plate.

2 Separate the eggs using a glass and plate, putting the yolks in a small bowl and the whites in a large bowl.

3 Melt the chocolate: put it in a medium bowl. Then stand it in a large bowl that has about 3 cm hot water at the bottom until the chocolate melts. Lift the chocolate bowl out of the water. Stir the yolks, orange rind and cream into the chocolate.

4 Whisk the egg whites in the large bowl until they form soft white peaks. Stir a couple of spoonfuls of this into the chocolate mix, then stir in the rest with a gently lifting and turning movement.

5 Cut the oranges in half and with a teaspoon scrape out the pith. (Don't throw this away. Later, you can squeeze this gently in a sieve to get the orange juice, either to drink or to use in Golden Muffins, on page 1.)

6 Spoon the mousse into each orange half and place in the refrigerator to set.

★ Decorate the mousse with chocolate leaves if you wish. See page 16.

No, no, don't ask anyone to eat the orange peel! You can throw the empty shells away with a clear conscience, because the skins will rot down easily.

Christmas Celebrations

Christmas is a time for parties, Christmas decorations and presents. It's time to celebrate with your family and friends, to patch up any quarrels and to give gifts as a sign of friendship.

The Christmas festival is celebrated because of the birth of a baby called Jesus, about 2,000 years ago. Jesus was the person who began the Christian religion. The Bible story tells us how angels rejoiced that there would be peace on Earth because he had been born.

As a grown man, Jesus had a lot to say about how God wanted people to care for each other, and showed people what he meant by what he did. This included sharing food generously, preparing meals for his friends, and helping out at parties! At other times, he cheerfully went without food so he could spend time helping people in other ways.

What an example for Christmas celebrations today.

CHRISTMAS CAKE

You can make these fruity cakes well in advance of Christmas, and store them wrapped in greaseproof paper and kitchen foil in a cool, dry place. Ice them just a few days before you want them to eat or to give away.

You need to soak the fruit the day before you bake.

2 large bowls
mixing spoon
15 cm round cake tin or giant muffin tins
greaseproof paper
metal skewer
wire rack

150 g currants
150 g sultanas
100 g raisins
50 g chopped glacé cherries
50 g chopped mixed peel
150 ml apple juice
100 g butter
100 g sugar
2 eggs
125 g plain flour
5 ml cinnamon
2 ml cloves

Heat the oven to 140°C before you mix the cake.

Line your tins with grease-proof paper.

1 Put the currants, sultanas, raisins, cherries and peel in a bowl along with the apple juice. Leave to soak overnight.

2 The next day, put the butter and sugar in the other bowl and mix until creamy. Add the eggs and mix again.

3 Next, stir in the flour and spices.

4 Finally, tip in the fruit and any juice that is left. Stir together.

5 Spoon the mixture into your choice of tins. Bake the mini cakes for about $2^{1}/_{2}$ hours, or the large cake for about $3^{1}/_{2}$ hours.

6 To test whether your cakes are done, lift them carefully out of the oven on to a heatproof surface. Pierce with a metal skewer. If the skewer comes out clean, the cake is done. If cake mix clings to it, the cake needs to be cooked for longer. Leave to cool for 10 minutes, then lift out on to the rack until cold.

MARZIPAN

mixing bowl
sieve
mixing spoon
small bowl
fork
rolling pin
small saucepan
pastry brush

225 g icing sugar
225 g caster sugar
450 g ground almonds
2 ml almond essence
1 ml lemon juice
2–3 eggs
extra icing sugar
60 ml apricot jam
nuts and glacé fruit

1 Sift the icing sugar and caster sugar into the bowl. Add the ground almonds, almond essence and lemon juice.

2 Break the eggs into a small bowl and beat lightly with the fork. Then add the egg a little at a time to the other ingredients, mixing in between, until they make a stiff dough.

3 Sprinkle a little extra icing sugar on a clean work surface and over the rolling pin. Roll out the marzipan to 3 mm thick. Then cut a large piece to cover your cake like a tablecloth, and smooth it down.

4 Heat the apricot jam in the saucepan until it is runny. Brush it over the top and sides of the cake

and cover these with marzipan.

★ While the marzipan is soft, add a mosaic decoration of chopped glacé fruit and nuts. Brush the part you want to cover with more apricot jam, press the fruit and nuts in place, and brush with still more apricot jam.

Easter Treats

Easter morning, and you're well into your umpteenth chocolate egg. What on earth is the reason for eggs and chicks?

In the northern parts of the world, the ancient spring festival was all about new life. In springtime there are bright new plants breaking out of dull-coloured seeds, and fragile chicks pecking their way out of eggs as lifeless-looking as stone.

At this time of year, about 2,000 years ago, there was another remarkable promise of new life. Jesus, the man who began the Christian religion, had been put to death; but 3 days later, on Easter Day, his grave was empty, and he was seen alive again. He had claimed to be God's Son, come to set people free. Now his promise had come true: his followers would also triumph over death. No wonder Christians are glad at this time!

In the Christian year, Easter also marks the end of a period of fasting, called Lent. As a result, Easter has become a time to enjoy some celebration foods.

TRUFFLE EGGS

small bowl

sieve

spoon

plate

small paper cases

50 g yoghurt cheese or cream cheese

50 g icing sugar

25 g cocoa

50 g ground almonds

chocolate vermicelli

1 Put the yoghurt cheese in a bowl and beat to soften.

2 Sieve the icing sugar into the bowl along with the cocoa. Mix.

3 Stir in the ground almonds and mix into a stiff paste. Chill in the fridge for 30 minutes.

4 Sprinkle the vermicelli on a plate.

5 Shape marble-sized pieces of the mixture into little eggs and roll in the vermicelli. The mixture makes about 30. Place each one in a paper case and refrigerate.

CHOCOLATEY CAKE

grater
mixing bowl
mixing spoon
small bowl
fork
sharp knife
20 cm round cake tin
5 ml oil
greaseproof paper
wire rack
small saucepan
spoon for mixing

1 small orange
175 g margarine or butter
175 g soft brown sugar
3 eggs
100 g self-raising flour
75 g wholemeal self-raising flour
275 g plain chocolate
300 ml double cream

Pre-heat the oven to 180°C.

Lightly oil the cake tin and line it with a circle of greaseproof paper.

1 Make sure the orange has been washed, then grate the rind into the mixing bowl.

2 Add the margarine to the bowl and beat with the mixing spoon to soften. Add the sugar and continue beating until the mixture is pale and fluffy.

3 Break the eggs into a small bowl and beat lightly with the fork. Add the beaten egg a little at a time to the mixture, beating thoroughly.

4 Spoon the flour into the mixture and stir in gently.

5 Cut the orange in half and squeeze out the juice. Add enough of the juice to make a soft mixture that drops off the spoon with a nice splodge.

6 Put the mixture into the tin and level the surface. Bake for about 40 minutes. By then the cake should have risen nicely.

7 Carefully lift it out of the oven. The centre should feel springy if you touch it with your fingertips. If it seems wobbly, carefully put the cake back in the oven for a few minutes more.

8 When the cake has cooled in the tin for a minute, turn it out on to a cake rack to cool.

9 Now make the icing: Put the cream in the small saucepan and heat on the top of the stove until you see the first little bubbles that show it is close to boiling point. Carefully lift the pan off the stove on to a heatproof surface.

10 Break the chocolate into pieces and add it to the pan. Stir until the chocolate has completely melted and the icing is smooth.

11 Let the icing cool, stirring occasionally. When it is thick and cold, put the cake on a serving plate and pour the icing over it so that it coats the top and sides.

12 Decorate with fresh flowers, if there are any growing in your area at Easter time, or with your own eggs made from truffle mix or marzipan (page 18).

Gift of Food

At Christmas, Christians remember how wise men from the East brought presents for Jesus. They remember all the presents that God has given them, including the gift of food from the world he made. At this special time of celebration, and throughout the year, they enjoy sharing this gift with other people.

There are many gifts of food that you can make using ideas in this book, to offer as a sign that you love and care for others.

More than that, by showing you and your family ways to have great food that is not too expensive throughout the year, you may be able to save some money to share with other people in the world who might otherwise go hungry.

Enjoy good food and make the world a fairer place: now that would be simply wonderful.

Make a shallow cardboard box with a lid—or cover an old one with paper. Line it with a paper doily and make a gift of home made biscuits.

Cut a circle of bright fabric or paper and tie it round a pot of home-made jam or ketchup.

Put some roast nuts in a cellophane bag and tie with colourful string.

GINGERBREAD GOODIES

saucepan
spoon for stirring
mixing bowl
mixing spoon
rolling pin
cookie cutters
2 baking trays
greaseproof paper

75 g brown sugar
30 ml golden syrup
15 ml black treacle
15 ml water
100 g margarine
5 ml cinnamon
5 ml ginger
2 ml cloves
250 g self-raising flour

Pre-heat the oven to 180°C.

Line the baking trays with greaseproof paper.

1 Put the sugar, syrup, treacle, water and margarine into a saucepan. Melt over a low heat.

2 Carefully lift the pan on to a heatproof surface and stir the mixture until smooth.

3 Mix the flour and spices together in a bowl. Carefully pour in the syrup mixture and stir until you have a firm dough.

4 Chill the mixture for about an hour.

5 Sprinkle extra flour on a clean work surface and roll the dough out to about 3 mm thick. Cut into shapes, and lift these carefully on to the lined baking trays. You can gather up your scraps and re-roll until all the dough is used up.

6 Bake the biscuits for 10 minutes, or until lightly puffed and just dark at the edges. Leave in the trays to cool and go hard before removing them.

★ Make stiff icing with icing sugar and egg white and use it to stick decorations on your finished Gingerbread Goodies.

★ Use a drinking straw to cut a hole in some shapes before you bake them. Later, you can thread yarn through this hole and hang your shapes on a Christmas tree.

Fill a box with a mixture of truffles and marzipan shapes. Nip off pieces of marzipan and dip one end in melted chocolate.

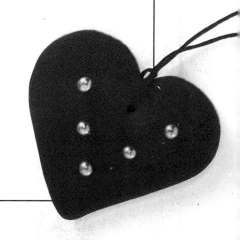

RECIPES

Apricot Toast   8
Banana Foam   2
Basic Bread   4
Beanfeast   12
Better-Than-Ketchup   9
Carrot Soup   11
Cheese Machine   5
Cheesy Crackers   14
Chocolate Leaves   16
Chocolate Oranges   17
Chocolatey Cake   19
Christmas Cake   18
Cinnamon Buns   3
Flower Power Salad   7
Fossil Floaties   14
Fruit Gondolas   1
Fruit Soup   3
Gingerbread Goodies   20
Golden Muffins   1
Lemon Mystery   13
Lemonade   14
Marzipan   18
Meatburger   10
Nice Rice   12
Oaties   2
Peanut Butter   6
Potato and Leek Soup   11
Raspberry Jam   6
Ratatat Stew   7
Red²   8
Saucy Chicken   15
Spicy Fruit Crumble   13
Spicy Sauce   15
Strawberry Ice   16
Sunshine Pizzas   17
Super Softies   4
Super Sweet Pickle   9
Surprise Eggs   15
Traditional Roast Nuts   6
Truffle Eggs   19
Vegetable Dip   17
Veggyburger   10
Very Vanilla   16
Vitamin Bottle   12
Yoghurt Plant   5

USEFUL FACTS AND FIGURES

Dry measures

grams	ounces
25	1
50	2
75	3
100	4
125	$4^1/_2$
150	5
175	6
200	7
225	8
250	9
275	10
300	11
325	$11^1/_2$
350	12
375	13
400	14
425	15
450	16 (1 lb)
475	17

Liquid measures

ml	spoonfuls
1	$^1/_4$ teaspoon
2	$^1/_2$ teaspoon
5	1 teaspoon
10	2 teaspoons
15	1 tablespoon

ml	fluid ounces
25	1
50	2
75	3
100	4
125	$4^1/_2$
150	5 ($^1/_4$ pint)
175	6
200	7
225	8
250	9
275	$9^1/_2$
300	10 ($^1/_2$ pint)
325	11
350	12
375	13
400	14
425	15 ($^3/_4$ pint)
450	16
475	17
500	18
525	19
550	20 (1 pint)

Oven temperatures

°C	°F	Gas
100	200	$^1/_4$
110	225	$^1/_4$
120	250	$^1/_2$
140	275	1
150	300	2
160	325	3
180	350	4
190	375	5
200	400	6
220	425	7

Eggs

These recipes were tested using size 3 eggs.

NOTE: Always check with a grown-up before doing any cooking.